RAISING WELL-BEHAVED PARENTS

THE FAMILY-SURVIVAL GUIDE FOR TEENS

A no-nonsense field guide to getting your way
in a world that's ruled by adults

HANAAN ROSENTHAL

TMI Publishing, Providence, RI
www.tmipublishing.com

to my awesome kids
olivia and aylam

Look for *"How Parents Think"* on Facebook

©2014 Hanaan Rosenthal
Too Much Information Publishing
61 Doyle Avenue
Providence, RI 02906
www.tmipublishing.com

Big thanks to Rage art and ragemaker.net for allowing me to create hillarious illustrations for this book!

ISBN: 978-1-938371-04-2

FAM034000 FAMILY & RELATIONSHIPS / Parenting / General
FAM043000 FAMILY & RELATIONSHIPS / Life Stages / Teenagers

Table of Contents

1

Before you send your parents to boarding school

Life can sometimes be drab and unfair, and whenever you look around to see who's in charge, it is hardly ever you. It's usually a parent, a teacher, coach, counselor, or other self-proclaimed responsible (whatever that means) adult.

Where is that justice everyone seems to be throwing around? Could it be that they mean it when they say "Life is not fair"?

It may seem sometimes that your life is a constant struggle between making unsuccessful attempts to make other people happy, and fighting for every inch of freedom you have.

It doesn't have to be that way.

You can, and must, take back your life. It is yours, and has always been yours, only now you're finally at an age where you can start owning it.

This book is not about planning a coup, overthrowing your parents' tyrannical rule, or taking over your house by force. It's not about to show you better rebellion strategies, or agree with you about how everyone else sucks. It is about showing you how you can greatly expand the room you have to maneuver as your life happens. It is about how to slowly but surely make your life yours, and keep it that way, while everyone around you cheers. Sure—your parents (and other adults) are controlling a lot of what is going on, but that doesn't mean that you don't have a say! In the same way that your parents say "No" to some things, they can also say "Yes." It is all in what exactly you ask for and how you ask for it.

Owning your life and doing more of what you want is your given right. It doesn't have to be a daily battle. It is all a matter of approach, perspective, and some inside understanding of how adults think, what they want, and how to give it to them without compromising your dignity or your objectives.

You will learn that you don't get more by demanding more. You don't get agreement by building a fortress. Once you get on the same page as the adults around you, they will also get on the same page you are on.

We will talk about adults, how they think, why they act like they do, and what they ultimately want.

But this book is not only about the way adults relate to you, it's also about how you relate to yourself. The way you think and what you believe, how you react to situations, and how you deal with your own emotions can make a huge impact on your life. We will go into those subjects in depth, and what you will find out will liberate you. I just know that.

Having it together

Adults like to behave as if they have it all worked out. They believe that if they can hold a job and pay the mortgage and insurance, they certainly can deal rationally and reasonably with easy stuff such as parenting.

The opposite can't be more true.

A lot of what adults do as parents, how they react and what makes them behave the way they do is far from controlled, rational behavior.

Parenting adults are many times lost and confused, and they react to situations in a way they wish they didn't. Many times they parent similarly to the way they were parented themselves, which makes them feel guilty. Then, they start acting out of guilt, which does not help matters at all.

Somewhere, your parents are acutely aware that they are messing up your life, and that by now it is far too late to fix anything.

Of course that is not always true—many parents do a great job, and a part of doing a great job as a parent is always feeling that you can do better. Still, parenting can come with a healthy dose of guilt about all the things we did wrong, and how it affected your life.

What you can do

Your goal is not to look for fairness in the world. Your job is not to be bound by your situation.

Your job is to figure out what you want your life to be, and then arrange things around you to get it that way. Understanding your parents, teachers, and other authority figures is a big part of that since they can grant permission and finance a lot of what it'll take.

You may want a new camera. You may want to take a special course in school reserved for older students. You may want a later bedtime or to stay out longer with friends. You may want to start driving or even have your own car, or get a job, or not have to get a job. All those things may require some adult consent. I will show you what to do in order to get a "Yes" much more often.

Why this will work

Your success and happiness reflects on those adults that surround you. When you are happy there's one less thing they have to worry about. When you do well, there's one more thing they can brag about. It may be annoying some-times, but understanding those facts can really help you in this point of your life.

When you are armed with knowledge of how adults think and what makes them say "Yes" or "No," your ability to live your life on your own terms is greatly enhanced. When you learn that parents, teachers, relatives, and other people around you want to give you their time, their atten-tion as needed, and yes, also their money, and you are willing to tweak your responses and attitude to work on your behalf, you can make big things happen.

You have everything you need around you. People that have been a sore in your life can become your cheerleaders. The best news is that you can do all that without compromising your values or ideals.

Let's figure out, together, how to make this the best darn life you can live. Let's decide to cut blaming and complaining, and take a step forward.

Let's stop complaining about your parent's deplorable behavior and instead give them the guidance they need.

Let's have you own this life of yours. Starting now.

2

A fresh look at success and failure

"I honestly think it is better to be a failure
at something you love than to be a success
at something you hate." George Burns

It seems as if from the day we can understand anything, we understand that what we want is to succeed. We also understand quite well that we want to avoid the opposite: failure.

But the search for success didn't include a manual or an orientation. No one ever sat us down and gave us the "success" talk, or gave us an initiation ceremony, welcoming us into this time-tested institution that everyone seems to want a piece of.

As clearly as we all know that what we want more than anything else is to succeed, we are all[1] rather confused about what success is.

It's as if everyone on earth was told of a treasure, was told to go and look for it, but was never given a map, a location, or a clear explanation of what to look for! Everyone seems to be running around trying to be successful, but hardly anyone dares to stop and ask: "Wait a minute . . . What am I looking for? What is success?"

This book is about success, but not the kind of success you might be familiar with. To understand what this means, lets look at two things we all want:

1. To have awesome things and amazing achievements.

2. To feel really great!

We mess up, not because we don't know what we want. We mess up because we don't know which one of those comes first.

Most people naturally believe that first we have to get things and achieve things, and then, naturally, we will be really happy about it.

Unfortunately, this is completely the other way around, and this book is here to show you just that.

Anything and everything that is worth having in the world can come to you through being just the person you were meant to be: free, happy, and content.

---

1   *Kids and grownups!*

What we all look for

Before we dive further into things like real-world success, or success in school and work, lets take a peek at another aspect of our lives: ***survival***.

When we're born, we are totally clueless about how things in the world work. We have no idea how to stay alive and how to get ahead.

Luckily, there's Mom, and possibly also Dad,[2] who are supposed to know their stuff. Our instincts tell us, and rightfully so, that in order to survive and thrive, we should look to see what those people that feed us do, and how they do it. Once we see what those trusty big-people do, we try to mimic them. But how do we know when we get it right? Nature must have set up a way for the grownups in charge to let us know if we're on the right path.

Nature[3] did, and in the process, it created a monster!

A monster named Approval

When we are in the process of growing up, the adults around us use their approval to guide our way. It's no wonder that getting approval from parents or other authority figures can make our day, or sometimes make our heart sink. We are designed to be deeply affected by approval, because earlier in our lives, our little selves depended on it so greatly.

Approval plays such a big part in our lives as humans that we all take great pleasure from positive feedback, far

---

2   *Or . . . two moms or two dads!*
3   *Or the universe, or god—whatever you want to call it.*

beyond the point where we should really care what other people think of us. Some of us keep looking for approval until the day we die. Many books and movies use that point to create some great drama. In **The Two Towers**, Tolkien has Faramir take his men to their certain death only to get approval from his father. He says: "When I return, think different of me, Father." He has no such luck.

While approval is a brilliant method of shaping us and preparing us to be able to take care of ourselves, it has one basic flaw: what do *we* do when the people who are supposed to use it to teach us are just as confused?

What adults think about success

So we established that as kids (and sometimes also as adults) we all look for approval. Regardless of whether we want it, need it, or whether our parents are qualified to give it. For the first conscious years of our lives, we all seem to be deeply affected by it.

But do the adults that wield their power of approval to shape our lives know where they are leading us? Do they even know where they are heading themselves? And if they do, do they ever stop for a minute between work, dishes, and arguing about curfew to ask themselves whether they are making progress, or even whether they are on the right path?

Sadly, most of us just don't.

It's one of those really crazy things. Think about it: millions of adults are walking around as if they own the place, acting as if they are in control, and dispensing swift judgment whenever possible, it seems. But all that, without a clearly thought-out purpose!

I personally like to assume that when someone is the captain, he or she knows where the ship is heading and why. I also like to see them pick up the compass once in a while and tweak their heading.

Hold on a minute—did I just say that there's a compass? Wouldn't that sort of solve everything? A universal way that tells us whether we're on the right track and heading in the right direction would surely save a lot of time and effort. But is there such a thing?

The good news, is, yes. Unlike Beckett from Disney's **Pirates of the Caribbean**, we don't have to chase a mentally unstable pirate across the ocean in order to find it. In fact, we each have our own compass.

Learning how to use our compass, however, is not that easy.

In a way, helping you to find your own compass and learn how to use it is in large part why I wrote this book.

But before we start looking, we have to figure out a few basic things, such as what we hope that compass will lead us to.

What's the point, anyway?

We eat, sleep, do homework, and play soccer. OK, so your soccer may be ballet, knitting, or electric guitar.

We know why we eat and sleep, we do homework because we are told to, and we play soccer for various reasons.

But if all that stuff we do is what makes up life, then I have a question for you: Does life by itself have a point? Is there a grand purpose to us all being here on this space-rock?

Some adults are a bit taken aback by this question. It's not only that most adults have no idea what our purpose is, but many don't believe that there's even such a thing as **purpose**, or even seriously thought about it in the first place.

Your life purpose is a big thing. Some can spend years without really understanding what it is. No worries, though. When it's the right time, you'll find out what it is. At this point in the book, I'm less interested in *what* your purpose is.

Right now lets focus on your everyday life.

When you grow up . . .

If your life is like the life of many other kids or teens, a lot of your focus is placed on what's coming next: next week's exams, next year's classes and freedoms, going to college, one day getting a driver's license, and of course, the all-mighty being a grownup and getting a good job. Sometimes it may seem that this is the grandest purpose of them all. After all, isn't the whole point of being a kid learning how to eventually be an adult?

I can answer that question for you with utmost certainty—it is not.

Believing that *what will come next* is going to be better than *how it is right now* is missing the point. It is like believing that the grass is greener on the other side, only to realize that if you got to the other side, you would realize that there's another place with greener grass yet. The same is true as we make our way through life: no matter where we are, we tend to believe that the next thing will be better.

But what is really wrong with looking forward? Isn't it exciting to move up on the ladder? Is wanting what's next such a big problem?

Looking to have more and better than what you have now is natural, and there's nothing wrong with it. How else would we ever grow if we didn't think bigger? But living in the future while believing that your present is somehow lacking is a problem. Lets see how.

First, *what is* is all there is—there is nothing else! Who you are right now and where you are right now is all you have. Even when you get to the next thing, it will still be *now* and it will still be *you*. A bit taller and a bit hairier,

13

but still the same you. You will not get ***there*** and say: "Ah, finally I am here!" Rather, you will say: "Hmm . . . Next year will be great because . . ."

Second, believing that things will be better when (fill in the blank[4]) is a chronic condition—there are many grownups that still believe that at some point in the future things will be good. Guess what—that time does arrive, but do things get better? Nope. There are new problems, new expectations, and new things to want instead.

When we live life waiting for the next big thing, we are missing out on the best part: life!

Life is happening here and now. You are a talented, awesome, complete person right now. You are not an "adult-in-training," you are not ***going*** to be this or that—you ***are***, today.

What you want to be when you grow up is fun to think about, but what I want you to think about even more is what you are right now. What you like doing today—what makes you happy, what makes you feel that you are creating something great. Those are the important things that will make your life feel amazing!

---

4   *When you . . . get through this year, go on vacation, start high school, get to senior year, get to college, have a job, etc.*

3

What makes you perfectly happy

*"Don't ask what the world needs. Ask what
makes you come alive and go do it. Because
what the world needs is more people who
have come alive"* ——*Howard Thurman*

Between all the things you have to do because you
were told to, like go to school and do chores, and things
you do because you're addicted to them[5], like TV, Xbox,
and Facebook, there's little time left to do things that
make you truly happy.

I know that this may be the case, and that you may not
even have a chance to figure out what it is that makes you
happy. I also know that it is important that you figure it out.
Let me try to explain why.

---

5   *Don't worry—so am I , , ,*

Those things that we love to do and are also good at will make us happy and fulfilled for the rest of our lives! Other people may have plans for you. Your parents may want you to be a lawyer or a doctor. They may want to make sure you are interested in things that will make you enough money, and that is nice. But when you get to do what you truly love to do, your life is certain to be fun and interesting. It doesn't have to be boring. The fun doesn't have to start after you finish work. The fun can start when you get to the office, or workshop, or field, or trail, or garage . . .

We will talk about that part much more. All I want you to understand for now is that what others expect from you is not at all as important as what you, yourself, want from your own life. Other people may have more life experience, but you are the only one that knows how to be you. Being you is a very unique job, and you were hired to do it from the day you were born.

Lets talk a bit more about funny things people believe.

No pain, no gain

Many people believe that in order to get anywhere in life you have to spend a lot of time doing things you don't like. You have to work hard, do things that you'd rather not, or just be bored. While some annoying stuff is unavoidable, I am convinced that living a life where you do what you like is much nicer. It is nicer at any point. It is nicer now that you are a kid, and it will be nicer later when you grow up.

You may hear that doing things you like to do has to come *after* you do the things you *have* to do. But somehow, as if by magic, the things we have to do end up filling our day, our week, our year, and eventually, our entire life. And why do we have to do those things? Partially, because they make other people happy. By the time you are done making other people happy, you have just enough energy to crash on the sofa and watch some TV.

What you love to do—that thing you are good at—has an important purpose in life. Somehow in our western society we tell kids to forget about what they love. We tell kids that what they love is not important, and that they can spend time doing it after they are done with important things like schoolwork and chores.

That is just plain wrong!

> **What you love to do, even if you haven't figured it out yet, has the potential to do something magical: it can allow you to find happiness for the rest of your life.**

Some of us have a very clear idea of what it is that we love to do. Some of us need some time to figure it out. The most important thing to remember is that it can be almost anything! It doesn't have to be something grand, it doesn't have to be the thing you will carry on doing when you're a grownup, and it doesn't at all have to be something that will start your career. It just has to be something that makes **you** feel fulfilled. It may or may not hint at what you will want to do later in life, but there is no telling what will happen later in life. While school is important for your future in some ways, your **now** is also important for your future. Only by finding time now, as a kid or teen, to delve into your own hobby and get excited about something that

17

is just yours, will you be able to carry that same feeling and excitement throughout your life.

Imagine that you are done with college, and get a job, and spend some time at that job, and suddenly you have some free time. Are you then going to figure out what you want to do with your free time to make yourself happy? That will be very difficult. Being happy is like any other part of your brain: if you don't keep it active, it will be rather difficult to figure it out later on.

So put this in the back of your mind: ***there is something I am good at, and I will figure it out and find time to do it***.

It is important, it is possible, and I will help you as much as I can with this book.

What you are good at

There are things about being human that we all share. Obvious things. We all have ears, and most of us can hear things. We can see, speak, smell, and dream.

We also know that there are some kids who are either very smart or talented. We call them names (nice names . . .) such as Artistic or Genius. What you may not know is that there is no such thing as a person, at any age, who has no talent! That's right—every person in the world, including you—has a talent. Every person is a genius at something.

There are those that know very well what they are good at, and those that have yet to figure it out.

If you are reading this now, that means that you are human, and that means that you also have some incredible talent, whether you know it or not. There is something that you can do really well, and you also have a lot of fun doing it.

Hold on, what is all this stuff about fun? I thought this was going to be a serious book about getting ahead! Shouldn't I be getting away from fun and focus on serious things?

You may want to be more mature, but you do not want to be like most adults. See, we have it all backwards. We believe that the younger you are the more fun you should have, and slowly learn how to be a serious adult. This is nothing but a heap of nonsense!

Having fun is where its at

I don't mean that all your life you should lie around playing on your Xbox. This is not the kind of fun I had in mind, although that can be perfectly good sometimes.

The fun I had in mind is never forgetting what you love to do. The fun I want you to have means for the rest of your life, do something that makes you smile, every day! And if not every day, than almost every day. What I want for you is that when you grow up you will look forward to getting to your work place to play with whatever toys you have there.

Now do me a favor. Read this part and then cut it out of the book and put it in your journal or somewhere. This is for two reasons: First, you can look at it often in order to remind yourself of this important idea. Second, put it away so that no adult can see it. If they did, they are most likely going to sit you down and give you a stern talking to about how *in life you can't always have your way. You can't always have everything you want,* and that *very few people grow up to work at what they love.* I don't know if this is right or wrong, but all this stuff some adults are telling us has nothing to do with us! They are not trying to limit us, but rather spare us from disappointment, perhaps disappointment that they themselves felt.

What we need to do is know that doing a lot of what we love is not only a fun thing, but rather it is the future of you, your family, and the whole world.

OK, Hanaan, now you are a bit over the top. I can save the world by doing what I like?

Let me lay it out in front of you in very simple terms. Lay out what? Nothing more than the secret to life itself in logical terms anyone can understand:

1. *Being happy is the most important thing in the world. What else is there?*

2. *When you do things you love and are good at, you are happy.*

3. *When you are happy, people around you are happier.*

4. *Start infecting people with happiness and soon enough you'll start an epidemic!*

You might think that I am kidding or simply out of my mind. I am not. I am willing to stake everything I have on this. Do what you love and you will change the world!

No one majors in being happy

So how did it happen that so many kids and adults don't really have much time for doing what they like? How can it be that so many teens finish school without any idea what they want to do next? Some people get so lost they have to go to Thailand, the Grand Canyon, or somewhere remote like that to "find themselves." What I want for you is to not lose yourself in the first place.

If being happy is so important, then why doesn't my school teach a "How To Be Happy" class?

Schools don't teach you how to be happy because people forgot how important it is. People think that if you have a good job and can have enough money to pay the rent and buy food, happiness will come.

It might, but unless you tell yourself that being happy is an important thing all by itself, you may never find it.

If you are still doubting the whole happiness thing, just take a look at the alternative: unhappiness. Suddenly being happy doesn't look like such a bad idea...

I made a decision long ago that what I want most of all is to be happy. I wanted it more than things or money or a good job. What I found out was amazing: the more I found happiness, the more I also found other things I wanted, like money and good work, and most important, someone sweet to share my life with. Imagine that—I now write books!

Being happy is not something that happens once you get things in life, like a nice girlfriend or boyfriend, or a car, or an acceptance letter to a good college. Being happy is something that happens from the inside. Being happy is something that you can, slowly, get yourself to be.

But how can we be happy if we get sad without wanting to?

Right. You get upset, sad, furious, stressed, and all those things without being able to control them at all, or even stop them. You can never stop those things from coming altogether. But you can have them come less often, and have more things happen that make you feel good.

Another thing this book will help you with is training your mind to bring you more things that make you feel good and less things that make you feel bad.

But is it really up to me to make my life better? Doesn't life just

happen? I don't really think I can control life!

Right, you don't control life. You also don't control nature, but you can plant a tree and see it grow and make sweet apples that you can later eat!

Possibly the most important thing to learn is that you don't need to **control** things in order to have them go your way.

Quite the opposite. You have to **let go of controlling** them.

What is happiness

Happiness is like a nice place you get to visit once in a while. You know you can't stay there forever, but whenever you're there, everything seems to flow smoothly, and you feel good.

The more we learn about what gets us to that magical place, and the more we realize how important it is for us to be there, the more we get to visit. Visiting happiness can become something that you can also do later in life. If you don't learn how to get there now, however, how can you know the way later in life?

Most people believe that what they call **reality** is made out of events and things. "I have my house and my car, I am married, I am going to work, and this weekend I'm having a party. This is my life." It is not. What makes our reality is not what we do, but rather how we feel! Imagine two people sitting next to each other in the classroom. Same teacher, same time, same class, but one feels good and the other one doesn't. Even though their reality seems the same at that point, it is very different. Who would you rather be?

Life is not made of things, places, and events. Life is made of one thing: how we feel.

Throughout that book, how we feel is going to be our compass.

We don't control how we feel. Feelings are like rain: one minute you are dry and collected, the next, a storm comes out of the blue, and you're drenched to the bone.

What we do control is our reaction to how we feel, and our reaction to what we think.

Wait a minute! How can we react to what we think? If WE think, can we think about our own thinking? Doesn't it mean that there are two of us?

Yes, it sort of does. There are many ways that people look at the different parts that make up our personality, and our humanness. In this book we will look at two. To not leave you hanging, for now, let's take a peek:

> *One part of you is your ego, and the other is the observer. The ego yells, and the observer listens and reflects. The ego judges, and the observer quietly observes.*

Another related part of us that I want to briefly mention now is our subconscious. The subconscious is the part of us that is active all the time. The subconscious is the part that makes things happen in our lives on a daily basis. For instance, do you have to think about walking? Reading? Talking? The next time you are having a conversation with someone, notice that words come out of your mouth, you may be walking at the same time without even noticing, your lips move, you make facial expression you don't always intend to, you laugh at something funny, all without even trying. You don't tell your mouth to move—it just does. You don't plan out the words before you say them—they just come out. As you sit and have a conversation, your fingers reach for your cell phone and reply to a text—all that without any thinking!

This is the subconscious at work!

> *What you can be is aware. You can observe. You can pay attention as all those things happen to your body as if by magic.*

In the next chapter we will talk a lot more about the subconscious and its amazing powers, about how it can sometimes be a pain in the butt, and how it can be used to help us get things done.

4

You, and the other you

"Our subconscious minds have no sense of humor, play no jokes and cannot tell the difference between reality and an imagined thought or image. What we continually think about eventually will manifest in our lives." Robert Collier

I don't really know what to make of it, but I swear that sometimes there are two of me.

I bet it happens to you, too. You think to yourself, or say out loud something like: "I don't know what I'm doing" or "I know I shouldn't do that, but I end up doing it anyway." What is the meaning of this craziness? How can we not know what we are doing? How can we *know* we should not do something, and we really mean to not do it, but we do it anyway? Are there two parts of us—one that **wants** things, and one that **does** different things?

Well, sort of. Lets sort out all the different parts of us humans. This will help us make sense of things later in the book.

We are not separate

In the Western world, we like to think about things we see in the world as separate. Every person is an individual unit that can communicate with the world with sound, sight, and touch. That seems to be true, and certainly makes sense based on what we can see. But it is only a part of the story—a very little part.

Beyond what is visible to us, we are connected to each other, and to everything else in the universe. This is true whether you can see it or not, and if you are like most people, you can't really see it, though you might sometimes feel it.

Knowing that we are connected to anything doesn't have any real practical uses. In fact, it's the opposite of practical: If you stood in the middle of class and said: "We are all connected!" you would probably soon hear what the rest of the class thinks about that. I suggest that you not try it . . . Regardless, that connectedness is a powerful resource. We'll ge to that soon.

Our subconscious

When we are little, we often encounter situations that we are not quite ready to deal with. Situations such as being hungry (even for a little bit), or being away from Mom. While now we know that waiting a minute or two for lunch is not the end of the world, and that mom will come back to us, when we are smaller, it can be really scary.

Lucky for us, we have a protector: our subconscious.

Our subconscious is far smarter than us in many ways. For example, it can figure things out really quickly, although it doesn't always tells us what it has figured out. Our sub-conscious is entrusted with directing our little selves to where it's safe and where's there's food.

How does a baby know that crying will get his mom to feed him? How does a toddler sometimes seem like she can manipulate Mom or Dad to get attention? Aren't they supposed to be clueless? They are clueless in some ways, but their protector is hard at work animating them to get the two things they need in order to live and thrive: food and love.

Our subconscious is also the part of our mind that learns how to do things, and then does them for us really easily— things like walking and talking. You may think those things are easy, but they take a huge amount of coordination be-tween different muscles and body parts. If we had to think about our every move while walking, we wouldn't be able to take three steps without falling down.

Who is our subconscious?

So we learned that we have a really powerful part in our minds called the subconscious. Every person has one, and it can figure things out fast, and can see things that we can't see. It can read what other people feel by observing their body language, it can tell if the area we are walking in is dangerous and give us warnings, and it can do many other things that we would not notice otherwise—and when we do notice them, we are not sure exactly how we did.

But if our subconscious is not us, who is it, and who are we?

The subconscious is a part of us. A part that is connected to everything else in the universe. And if we call it the *sub*conscious, then we must be the ***conscious mind***. Conscious, as in being aware.

Our subconscious is about a million times more powerful than our conscious mind, and has access to everything we have seen and experienced since we were born.

Ok, but if a part of me knows all that stuff, why doesn't it help me during tests? Why can

I still know something but forget it, like someone's name?

Our conscious mind, as you'll probably agree, is rather stupid, at least in comparison to the amazing power of the subconscious. Our conscious mind gets distracted very often. It can't hold on to a thought for more than a minute of so without spacing out or wandering off to other thoughts, and can't even memorize a shopping list with more than ten items. Why then are we stuck with the stupid part of the brain when another part of us is so darn awesome?

To start, the conscious mind would simply not be able to handle the massive amount of information held in the subconscious. It would quickly get overloaded. Second, there are important things that we can do with our conscious mind that the subconscious can't touch.

What the subconscious can't do

With all its amazing powers, the subconscious lacks one key ability.

There is one thing that we can do with our conscious mind that the subconscious cannot:

We can imagine things that don't exist!

What? I get yelled at for imagining things!!

This ability to imagine may not seem like a big deal, and can even get us in trouble sometimes. After all, no one goes around encouraging you to dream! Kids dream too much anyway, don't they? They need to get their heads out of the clouds and plant their feet firmly in reality.

Wrong.

We all need to learn how to consciously use our imagination, because, simply put, it is the most pure creation tool we possess!

I know what you must be thinking. Isn't actually ***doing something*** an act of creation? Isn't dreaming just a waste of time?

We are about to figure it all out.

I understand that some of the things I am writing about might not exactly agree with what you know about life, and about how things happen. Bear with me, though—I promise it will be worth your while.

How things get created

I dare you to show me something you created that did not first exist in your imagination. There is no such thing.

Anything and everything you have ever created started out in the form of a thought. A thought of something you want that did not yet exist in the physical world. One way to look at it is to imagine that there are two worlds: The physical world where we all live, where there are things you can hold and streets to walk on, and your imagination world where you can create as many things as you want. The imagination world is in fact the rough draft for the future of the real world. Things you imagine don't always come to be, but there is nothing that you created that **didn't** start in the world in your imagination.

This world of imagination is what separates you from your subconscious. As powerful as your subconscious is, it can only act on things that your conscious mind imagines. Your subconscious can figure out almost anything, but your inspiration is **always** the spark. Your subconscious is your conscious mind's all-powerful and dedicated butler.

Your imagination on the other hand, is an amazing creation tool. It works by painting a picture for your subconscious to follow. The act of visualizing something as you want it is how everything is created. What happens after that are the details that we have little control over.

Can we stop creating?

We can stop creating as much as we can stop pondering future events.

We are constantly imagining things, but they are not always things that we really **want**. For example, being anxious about something going wrong is imagining. In fact, any time we think about the way we think things will turn out, we are using our imagination. It is not our fault, nor can we stop it. It is how we are built.

The machine that slowly transforms our beliefs into reality keeps working.

> *It's important to distinguish between thinking and believing. Our thoughts can affect our beliefs, and our beliefs can then affect the physical reality.*
>
> *A thought can never manifest and become reality as a result of you thinking it.*
>
> *The process of manifestation works surely and slowly.*

Our role then is not to stop imagining, or start imagining. **Our role is to imagine things the way we want them to be.** We can sometimes decide to stop what we are doing, sit down, and imagine something we want. This process of using the imagination to bring things you want into your life is called visualizing, and it is used by people everywhere to achieve amazing things they want.

This can be a bit stressful

Damn! If my thoughts create my reality, can

I hurt people
by thinking
bad things? Can
I ruin my life
by thinking the
wrong thing
by mistake?

No, you can't.

The first thing that happens as we begin to be aware of our ability to create is that we panic a bit. Some of us start to guard every thought and feel super anxious about the terror we can create in our lives if the wrong thought comes through.

This is not how it works.

Your reality is supported by other people and your past, and you can't just create horrible things for yourself. One thought, one bad mood, or one anxiety attack can't influence your life on its own.

Also, it takes several weeks to experience the effect of the sum of your thoughts because it is not your thoughts that affect your reality as much as your beliefs. Your thoughts affect what you believe much like your health is affected by what you eat. You can indulge once in a while without causing any disease, but if you eat crap every day, you will get sick eventually . . .

What we are looking to do is not get stressed, but rather the opposite! We are looking to simply create a few nice things. Whether your life is a bit of a mess or going OK, you can only improve it. So, settle down—you are not going to rain fire and destruction on yourself and your friends with the wrong thought.

Our ego

In order to help us out as we grow, our subconscious creates a little friend for us: our ego. Our ego is the one that tells us that we are separate from other things and people, and that the universe is a material place with separate people.

One of the tricky things about our ego is that it speaks to us in the first person. That's right, our ego thinks that it is us! Instead of saying, "Nothing will ever become of you," it says, "I shouldn't try." Instead of saying, "You have to be prepared," it says, "I will definitely fail the test."

So how do you know if the thoughts you are thinking are your thoughts or your ego's thoughts? It's not always easy, but here's one trick:

Since the main job of our egos is to protect us, you can identify your ego by the kind of thoughts it creates. Those are usually warning thoughts, thoughts that find crafty ways to tell us what we shouldn't be doing. Sometimes those thoughts are really important, like when we see a barking dog and think, "Stay away." But there are other kinds of warning thoughts that actually hold us back. Let's look at some of those thoughts and see what they are protecting us from.

When we first have this kind of thought: "I really like this girl/boy," our ego might responds with this thought: "I shouldn't go and talk to that girl (or boy) I like." Or if we think: "I want to sign up for art class," our ego might say: "Forget it, it's a bad idea . . ."

Notice how the response from the ego looks as if we are thinking it. We are not. It is like an automated message telling people that you are not available to pick up the phone. It sounds like us, but it is only an automated message.

This type of automatic ego-thought is protecting us from two things: being made fun of, and rejection! Rejection is a really scary thing. The fear that other kids will not want to hang out with us is one of the worst things. In reality, the fear of rejection is usually much worse than the actual experience of rejection. In reality, people who know us like us for being ourselves, and we end up worrying too much about things that don't really matter.

We also tend to want to do things that we believe will help us get accepted. There's nothing wrong with that. The problem starts when we do things that compromise who we are. For example, if kids push us to smoke, and we do it even though we know it is really bad for us, it's not a good thing. Now I know, you've heard it before a million times: "Smoking is not good." But this is not the same thing I am talking about. I am not referring to how bad it is for your body to smoke (or drink, or do anything that you feel you shouldn't), I am talking about compromising your integrity.

You are a person who knows what is right for you. There are people around you, even if you haven't noticed them yet, who would love to be your friend as you are. Real good friends don't ask you to be who you are not. They don't say things like, "If you want to hang around with us you have to do things you don't feel comfortable with." Good friends want you to just be yourself.

Your ego is the part of you that pushes you to be accepted at any price.

Procrastination

There are other type of thoughts that the ego plants in our mind. For example, procrastination. Why in the world do we procrastinate? Can you imagine a dumber thing that we do? And we **all** do it!

I know that studying for the exam is good for me, I even sort of like the material, and I know it will only take one hour and after that I can feel much freer. However, the subconscious has a different plan for you. It has your ego tells you things like: "There's something really good on TV that I have to watch right now," or "I just have to get another level in Skyrim."

Those thoughts can drag you in the wrong direction for various reasons. One common reason is that while we all admit that we are afraid to fail, there is another thing we are almost as afraid of: success! Sounds unbelievable? It is not. Success means that people will be expecting more from us. This is scary. Success means that people will start paying attention to us. Success means that our friends might make fun of us (depending who are friends are, of course).

What makes procrastination even more infuriating is that the subconscious can just as easily put thoughts in your mind that will make you sit down and finish your homework. Instead, it plants thoughts that make you decide not to get things done.

One thing is for sure: fighting procrastination is hard to do and almost never works. Later in the book we will look at real things we can do to melt away annoyances such as procrastination and other questionable things we do that we know are not beneficial.

The other you wants attention

When I grew up, my parents didn't always have a lot of time for me. I was raised on a kibbutz, which is a kind of an agricultural collective community. One of the unique things about growing up on a kibbutz back then was how children were raised. Instead of being raised, put to bed, and woken up by our parents, on the kibbutz all the children of the same age slept together in what we called a children's house. Imagine that: every night, 10–15 kids without any grownups! The life . . .

What we had in freedom, we lacked in attention from grownups, and especially from our parents. I remember that when I was growing up, getting attention was constantly on my mind. In order to get attention, I did things like make up unbelievable stories, and even steal. I also used to wet my bed until far after all my friends had stopped. It was then that I had my first encounter with my own subconscious. I was eleven, and really fed up with waking up in a wet bed every morning. Our teacher, Gillit, explained to me that it was my choice whether I wet my bed or not. "But how can I control what I do when I am a sleep?" I protested.

She explained to me that even though I can't really **control** what my body does when I am a sleep, I can tell my body what I expect of it, and the part that **does** control it, my subconscious, will follow my direction.

It didn't take long, and my assertive conversations with my own subconscious paid off. Within a month or so I was dry, and never looked back.

You see, although the behavior started because I was looking for attention, it got stuck there far past the time that it was needed. This happens with many things we do. Even though the reason we may do something is no longer valid, our subconscious is so used to doing it that stopping takes a lot of effort, and some creative ways.

That ability to tell my subconscious what I expect of it also served me well later in life. I wish I had put two and two together earlier because there are so many times in my childhood when I would have used this trick.

5

Behaviors of the common adult in its natural habitat

"To punish me for my contempt for authority, fate made me an authority myself." - Albert Einstein

If you are like most teens, you live in the unavoidable reality that adults control and dictate what you do in almost every hour of your life. Even when you are doing something that you want to do, it is only because someone older allowed you to do it.

This is not entirely bad. After all, it is the same people that make sure you have food, clean clothes, and a place to crash. They will most likely pay for your education, help you buy your first car, cook meals for you, and do your laundry far beyond the point that you can do those things yourself.

Your relationship with those adults can be a bit contentious. On one hand, you have a real sense that you can handle more responsibility and freedom, and on the other hand, it isn't always recognized.

This chapter is dedicated to helping you better understand those adults so that you can coexist with them better. Be it your parents, teachers, coaches, counselors, or other adult authority figures, knowing what they want and how they think, and acting accordingly, can smooth out your experience and leave you with less frustration and more of the life you want.

Autonomy

Definition of AUTONOMY:

self-directing freedom and especially moral independence

A self-governing state

Autonomy is one's ability to rule one's own life within a set of constraints.

For example, our ferret has a fully autonomous life inside his own cage. He can eat when he wants, sleep and wake up on his own schedule, and, well, do his business when and where he wants.

When he was smaller, he didn't know where to do his business, so he had less freedom. He was in a smaller cage and we paid attention to his every move. When he was going to the bathroom, we showed him where to go.

Now that he sort of gets it, he can even roam free in our bedroom.

Growing up in this adult-dominated world is a bit like that: You have some space for yourself and some freedom, but it is within the confines of what adults allow you to have! What you may want more than anything, and for a good reason, is greater freedom. Freedom makes us feel more capable, more trusted, more valued and appreciated. Too much freedom, however, can really mess us up. Too much freedom, as I had when I was growing up on a kibbutz in Israel, can leave you yearning for any adult supervision and for stricter borders.

The right amount of freedom is where you get enough attention and feedback, but at the same time are slowly given more responsibility and ability to manage more of your time.

This is not a book for your parents, though, so telling you that you may need more supervision or more freedom won't really help, and I will most likely be preaching to the choir.

What I am going to do is show you how you can, as a teen (or younger), do the only thing you can: slowly shift your situation in the direction you want it to go. Whether what you need is more freedom or more structure and supervision, it can slowly and surely be obtained.

Until you finish school and move out, you will most likely be supervised. However, expanding your autonomy within the confines of this supervision can make for a more enjoyable and productive time. The key to doing that is very simple: working to better understand those people that supervise you.

Let's get to it.

How adults parent

Adults like to pretend they have all their ducks in a row.

They do not.

Many of the reactions your parents have to things you do and ask of them come from what was done to them as kids by their own parents. Sure, they have their own twist on it because they are different people, but in many cases there is more instinct and less thinking. This, in an odd way, leaves you with more of an opportunity to make a difference.

Many times parents also act and react out of the need to protect you. This is the reason why the word "No" seems to come out of their mouth much more frequently than either "Sure, no problem" or "Let me think about it." Parents will sometimes say "No" before thinking things through. This can be a bit of a catch-22[6] because many adults aren't thrilled about changing their minds. Once the "No" spell has been cast, it is not easy to take it back.

---

6   *A catch-22 is a situation where no matter what you do, you will lose. For example, if you walk alone in the desert and carry a large tank of water, you are in a catch-22. If you need to walk in order to survive, you have to leave the water behind, which of course will make it much more difficult for you to survive.*

How parenting seems to you:

What's happening in the parent's head

Parents sometime feel that they have to act swiftly and show no hesitation. Sometimes, the more adamant and swift we are, it actually means that we are not totally sure of ourselves.

Many times parents say something and then regret it right away, as if it was something that was told to them when they were kids, and when the same situation came up with them being the parents, the same reaction they used to get as kids suddenly came out, and they are not sure exactly how.

Those are some of the reasons why you sometimes feel that your parents are not being fair. It's because sometimes they aren't.

What you have to remember is one important fact: even the most unreasonable people can actually be rather reasonable. What that means for you is that in order to get more verdicts in your favor in your home's very own family court, it really helps to change the way you approach the judges.

Managing your parents

You know how sometimes you just know that your parents are acting like unfair jerks? Well, this is because sometimes they are. Not all the time, and not every time you think that. Sometimes they have a very good reason to do something that makes you unhappy.

Nonetheless, as we know, parents are not perfect—they lose their cool, snap, punish unjustly, yell in public, etc. They always feel horrible about being unfair. The difference is that some of them know how to apologize and make it right, and for others it is more difficult.

You can't change your parents, so wishing you had different parents or that Mom or Dad would be less of this or more of that is really not up to you. However, you can make a significant difference. You have to realize that your parents' reactions to you or how they relate to you is a cycle that you are a part of. Changing your part of the play will also change the part of the other cast members.

Of course, when you set out to change your part in a way that more effectively manages your parents, you need to be subtle about it. If your parents feel manipulated, it can backfire! So you don't want to be manipulative, per se, but there are things that you could either do to make the situation more pleasant for you (and everyone else in the house), or on the other hand, not do.

It is tough to make blanket statements about how parents will react from where I am sitting, because every parent in the world is a bit different. However, there are some basic guidelines that should consistently help.

One of the things some kids do (without meaning to, of course) is catch their parents in situations where they know they will get a negative response. This is a part of the negative cycle. A subconscious part of us, believe it or not, is actually looking for conflict! This part does that out of habit, not out of wanting to cause trouble.

It takes a great amount of discipline not to blame someone for being "mean" to you, and instead look at what your role is. When considering this, it is important overall to not fall into the blame trap. Just as I want you to know that I am not blaming you for your parent's behavior, I urge you to avoid blaming your parents or blaming yourself.

When we blame, we don't get any closer to a resolution. Instead, we get further away from it. The key to your life moving forward and getting better is taking responsibility for your part, not looking at where others contributed to what is wrong with your life. This is true for you, your parents and everyone else.

Unfortunately, many adults as well as kids fall into that blame trap, fully believing that their life situation is someone else's fault. It may be so, but that is not the point. The point is that blaming makes things worse for you, not better.

I am not in any way suggesting that you are the one causing those situations, or that anything that happens in your family is your fault. You may contribute to the situation sometimes, of course, but family structure is too complex to find someone and accurately point a finger.

All you can do is decide to change your part in it as much as you can. You don't have to be the peace-keeper of the family. You don't have to be the one that is constantly trying to make everything OK for everyone else. What you do have to realize is that when you change your part in the family's equation, the result has to change as well.

The less you focus on what's fair or not fair, what you deserve and you don't get, and what your siblings get that you don't, the happier your life will be! What you can and should focus on is you! Focus on the things you like to do and the things that make you happy.

You can't stop needing your parents, and in most cases you shouldn't try. What you are responsible for is your own reaction—your own behavior, your own responses and attitude.

Woody Allen

There's a reason why I am referencing an old Jewish guy from Hollywood here—just give it a minute . . .

When my wife, Johanne, was growing up, her mom acknowledged her own mood swings and helped Johanne deal with them in a really creative way: humor!

She told Johanne that when she (her mom) got unreasonable and raised her voice and started all sorts of drama, Johanne should pretend she was watching a funny Woody Allen movie. See, Woody Allen is one of the funniest movie-makers that ever lived. He made great movies because he could capture how silly we all act and how dramatic and posing we can be. Through his movies, he helps us make fun of ourselves.

Having a sense of humor about your parents acting up can be an amazing step in keeping your sanity and composure.

Here's how my wife's mom communicated her advice: "Whenever I act crazy, just pretend we are characters in a Woody Allen movie. Now, never ever let me know that you are doing that. Remember, you are a part of the movie as well, but instead of getting upset by what I am saying, just laugh about it to yourself."

This advice saved my wife, as a kid, from many situations where her mom, when she was still an alcoholic, went over the top yelling at her. Now they look back at those times and laugh, but back then this way of thinking was very powerful.

We all act crazy once in a while. The key is not to buy into your mom or dad's temporary insanity. It's a curious thing, but a family is a lot like a TV show with a repeating theme: the fights and dynamics always seem to repeat. This can make it all the easier to make fun of.

Remember, though, do this only in your head. If Dad sees you chuckle while he's having his stupid fits, or Mom suspects that you are not taking her rants seriously, you will get in even more trouble. For those times, you have all the right to practice your acting skills!

Here's an example:

In the Gibson Residence, drama was flying high once again...

"This is the second time this month that I am finding my iPhone inside the couch! If you kids don't know how to put it back after borrowing it I have no idea what I'll do! You kids are just irresponsible freeloaders! You have no idea what it takes to make enough money to feed you, and the way I get rewarded is by having to spend my Sunday searching for my phone! Next time I find it somewhere like that there will be no TV for a week!"

Now, dad is obviously being a bit crazy after a long day at work. He's saying his bit, but he means very little of it, if anything. He's probably already regretting half of it . . .

Reaction 1 - Not knowing you are part of the show:

What is wrong: Buying into Dad's speech when he's obviously crazy doesn't help anyone and can be upsetting. Believe me, he most likely doesn't mean a word of it and just needs to get something off his chest.

Reaction 2 - Comedy act!

What worked here: You didn't let Dad know that you thought he was funny! You didn't take the threats, accusations, and somewhat mean comments to heart. You took responsibility at the end!

Taking responsibility may seem like a risky move. After all, it sometimes appears that denying will get you in the least amount of trouble. This may be true in the short term, but taking responsibility, especially for something you have done, is a much healthier thing to do in the long term. It helps your parents see that you are being more mature and eventually can handle more responsibility.

Taking responsibility makes you instantly more believable and trustworthy. In a way, messing up and then owning it is an opportunity to establish your credibility.

Authority figures want to be respected

Authority is not given, it is earned. Being an authority figure is not something anyone should take lightly. I believe that people that deserve their authority status should not earn it once, but keep on earning it. You can help them earn it by asking lots of questions. It's a way of keeping them honest.

For example, if you see your teacher dump an empty soda can in the trash, it is perfectly OK to ask them to use the recycling. You have questioned their authority. After all, they should know better than you where their empty containers go.

While I fully believe that authority should always be questioned, the manner in which this questioning happens is key. Sometimes that questioning should happen inside your head and never come out. Not because you should fear authority figures, but because when you are respectful you have a much better chance of getting your way.

Being respectful doesn't mean you have to become a "brown nose" or suck up to anyone. Actually, parents can smell when you suck up from a mile away and they can get suspicious instantly. Avoid!

Here are some examples of approaching parents in two ways:

Disrespect will never get you a sympathetic ear:

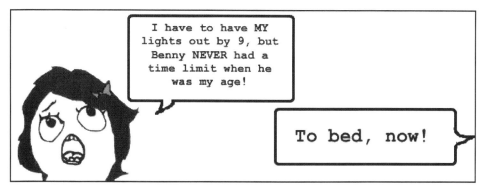

What was not helpful: Disrespectful tone = pissed Mom off. Comparing parenting of your siblings: Brrrr! Parents hate that! Also, the girl didn't ask for anything, she was just accusing. Here are some other options:

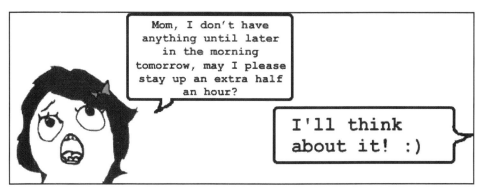

What was right: The girl didn't confront Mom, but rather let Mom feel that she respects her opinion.

The girl showed maturity by offering to do another chore, which Mom probably won't enforce anyway . . .

There's always a chance that Mom may say no, but you have not alienated her, and you have left the door open to ask again at some point. No matter what the answer is, appreciate it!

Parents want appreciation

Any time you possibly can during the day, and you find the appropriate opportunity, voice appreciation to your parents. This works better than fabric softener on an old towel. Don't lay it on thick, just a few words such as: "Mom, thank you for making me yummy food the other day for lunch," or "Dad, thanks for taking the time to come to my baseball game. It means a lot to me."

Little gestures like that are free for you, but they send out many positive ripples. First, showing gratitude brightens up everyone's mood! Every family can use that on any day. Don't you agree? Second, it means money in the bank as far as the next extra-curricular activity that may require parental cooperation.

Remember, parents are not machines, and they don't like to feel that taking care of you is a job. Anything you can do to verbally show that you don't take anything for granted (even if you need to make something up) can make a big difference. Think about chores you perform around the house. You do them because you have to, sure, but getting a pat on the back always feels great and makes you want to do a better job the next time. Adults are just the same. The more appreciated they feel, the better whatever it is they are doing for you will be.

Granted, taking care of you is not only your parent's job, it's the most important one they have. The nicer you are to someone whose job is to take care of you, the nicer they will treat you. Positive feedback works much better than negative feedback. This is true even if you believe they do a sucky job, as some parents do.

Remember—parenting can be a difficult thing. There's so much baggage, so much guilt, and so much subconscious behavior that contribute to your parents making all the wrong choices, so when they do get something right—boy, oh boy, you want to be all over that one!

Here's an example of how appreciation can help:

Finding something to be grateful about and expressing it may not come as naturally for all of us as finding something to complain about. However, making the switch and voicing appreciation always has a profound effect on how everyone feels, and the better people around you feel, the better everything else seems to be. Actually, the better everything else actually is!

Parents want to look good, mainly in public

> Are you asking that
> we pretend that
> everything is OK
> when it is not, just
> so that it makes
> a good show?

Ah . . . Yes, I guess this is what I am saying. But wait—there's a good reason for that. I am not asking you to make your parents look good for your parents' sake, but rather for your own good.

Unless you have a situation in which other people must intervene and help you (there's a section about that below), your issues with Mom and Dad should remain just that. Making a scene will aggravate any situation, and when a situation gets aggravated between you and your parents, everyone ends up feeling crappy, and you end up with an extra chore or a removed privilege.

Parents need to know that they have their ducks in a row and have all the information, or at least look as if they do. They need to know that they control the situation and that they don't look foolish. Whenever you can help with that, do what you can. It is sure to pay off.

Dad and son in grocery store

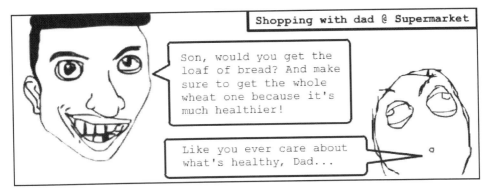

What was off: While you know that Dad usually doesn't care about the nutritional value of a slice of bread, and you caught him trying to impress strangers in the market, making a point of it may not be the best thing. We all try to show off once in a while and hate to have that pointed out.

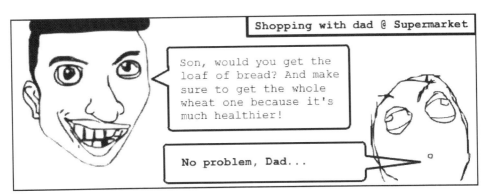

What worked: You kept the snarky (yet fitting) comment to yourself. Sharing it later with Mom may actually be rather funny and far less embarrassing, if you feel Dad can take that.

Learn to manage your expectations

As a teen, one of the toughest things to discover is that your parents are not perfect. I know, you must be laughing right now because you know of so many things your parents can do better! Regardless, we all, to some extent, want our parents to do the right thing, and we can be shattered when they let us down.

The fact is, when your parents were going to school, there was no "Parenting" course offered. All they know about parenting is what they got from their own parents, and what they picked up along the way.

Regardless of what they are messing up, there are two things you have to consider:

1. They are doing the best they can, even if it seems improbable.

2. You cannot cause them to change by being mad at them, revolting against them, or doing things that they told you not to just to get them back.

Some people change, and some don't. Some become better, and some worse. Most important, almost, is that most people, including your parents, have things they do really well and can be a lot of fun when they do!

Your job is two-fold, then:

Expect less from your parents in the areas you know they stink at.

Spend more time enjoying with them things they are good at!

Yes, it is their responsibility to do basic things such as telling you how great you're doing, knowing when you're upset and giving you some slack, spending time with you doing things you like, etc. However, some of them just can't. At some point you would want to give up on that, or disappointment is going to be a bigger and bigger part of your life. It is perfectly **OK** to decide that you can do without some basic things your mom or dad are just bad at giving you.

It's not that you are letting them off the hook, but rather that you are letting yourself off the hook. You are allowing yourself to just be a person. You are letting yourself enjoy what your parents can give, and letting go of what you want but that you know will only bring more frustration and letdown.

Here are some examples:

Waiting on the steps at school for dad to pick him up

Kid looking from kitchen seeing Dad watching baseball

What went right: The kid obviously figured out what his dad's drawbacks are and decided not to get too bent out of shape about them.

He also figured out how to find things to do with his dad that will allow them to hang out together.

Yes, indeed—we sometimes have to parent our own parents. It may be unfair, but we are not looking for justice; we are looking to make our life nicer!

Being told "No"

It sometimes seems that you know when a "No" is going to come even before it does. A part of you is already working on the revolt speech.

Stop. Think about what you are looking to achieve.

Sometimes we need a reason to be upset, and that's a perfectly good way: You ask for something you can't have (in a slightly unpleasant manner), you're told "No," and you get upset. You can go tell your friends how mean and unreasonable your parents are and have a really good rant—nothing wrong with that.

However, when your goal is not to test the boundaries and add to life's drama, but to actually get a "Yes," there are things you can do to increase your chances.

There are some things you can do before you ask, and even some things you can do after you get the "No," in case you do.

Here are some "No" rules:

If you believe that you're most likely going to get a "No," then just drop it! Getting a "No" for one thing does not improve your chance at a "Yes" later on. When your parents tell you "No" for anything, they somewhere feel bad because some part of them would like to give you everything. So "No" causes some guilt and should be avoided if you know it's inevitable.

A "No" is almost never final, no matter what your parents say! There's always something you can do to convert a "No" into a "Yes."

For important matters where you really want a "Yes," make sure to ask for a delayed answer. Parents take you much more seriously and are much more likely to say "Yes" when you are patient.

If the deciding "No" vote has already been cast, then it's time to go into triage mode. See Managing Concerns section later on.

Appreciate, respect, and be grateful equally for a "No" as you would be for a "Yes."

Why in the world would I appreciate a «No"?

Because, if you can't change it, showing your parents respect can only benefit you in the long term. When your parents don't feel judged, they are much more likely to think about things longer and more creatively, resulting in more "Yes."

Managing Concerns

Behind every "No" you get, there's a concern.

While I would strongly deter you from going against what your parents say, I would very much encourage you to take that matter further and not see the initial refusal as the final word.

The way to do that is by starting an official inquiry!

Start by imagining what possibly could be the reasons for them telling you "No," and think about ways that you can work with it.

Never ever say things like "But (whatever they worry about) won't happen" or "You just don't trust me". Remember, your goal is not showing your parents that they are dumb and you are smart (although that is a great sport!). Your goal is to have them change their mind.

Find a quiet time and start a conversation that will go something like this:

"Mom (or Dad), I want to talk about that camp again. I know you said 'No,' and I respect that, but I want to know what your reasons are so that maybe there is something I can do to make it into a possibility."

Now, regardless of how infuriating the answer may be, or how final, you always have a chance! Think about the possibilities: If it's money, suggest paying a token amount from your own money. Suggest doing chores or babysitting or something. You don't necessarily have to make a significant dent in the price, but you are going to show just how serious you are about it. You will show that you are not just asking and asking, but that you're also willing to give and be a part of making it happen—a trait appreciated by parents all around!

If the concern is safety, ask what you can do to calm her concerns: "There will be a parent supervising us all the time," "I will be sharing a room with my girlfriends (if you're a girl)," or "I will be sharing a room with Joey the whole time, and he hates smoking as much as I do!"

Whether you changed her mind or not, this was a worthwhile exercise. You showed her respect, you showed maturity, you showed that you can discuss things without having a fit or being upset. You made yourself a reasonable and useful party in the process, and that is going to be very helpful in the long run. You created valuable goodwill from one of your life's deciders by understanding how they think and acting in a way that gets results, rather than a way that may seem right but only gets everyone frustrated. Good work!

6

Family matters

*"The best way to get a puppy is to beg for
a baby brother—and they'll settle for a
puppy every time."* Winston Pendelton

Most of your interaction with your parents happens around the house, and no matter where you live, the themes and problems are almost always the same.

In this chapter we will be looking at some of those themes that kids find themselves grappling with in regard to their parents. We will look at the family structure and how you can build yourself a respectable place within it.

Talk back without talking back

One of the classic things parents can't stand, and for a good reason, is talking back. This ties into the need of parents to feel respected, appreciated, and in charge.

This should help illustrate the subtle differences between having a constructive conversation and talking back:

It was witty, and will crack up and impress your friends, but too bad you will not get to see them very often as you have just alienated your prison warden.

Mom: Sure, go ahead.

I will be back before 11 so that I get a good night's sleep, and you know none of my friends drink. We will be at Johnny's house and his parents are there so no funny business. I'll give you a call as soon as I get there and right before I leave.

What worked? Everything! You showed respect. You dealt with several potential concerns your mom had. You showed that you understand and regard her concerns seriously. You were mature and trustworthy. This is a sure way to build trust for future events.

Being a smart-ass will not get you to be any smarter, and doesn't make you look smarter either. It will get you less of the things you want and more of the things you don't. It may seem cool to defy your parents and show them who the boss is. My strong advice to you: it is not cool. It is pointless. It is immature. Let that part of your life go. Your mom or dad may not be the coolest people in the world. In fact, from time to time, they can seem like a pair of clueless people that provide a constant source of embarrassment.

Regardless, you are stuck with them, and they are responsible for you.

Work with them. Find out what language you do have in common with them. If your friends think you're a loser for getting along with your parents, then it can only come from one place: they are jealous.

Picking your battles

You can't have everything, therefore you should not ask for everything. You should not make a stink about everything and you should not make a point about everything you want that you can't have.

It sounds like it would make sense to try and get as many things your way as possible, and with this approach you are surely going to get more than if you just ask for a few. This is not the way it goes down. The things you do choose to request special permission to do need to be carefully picked. If you ask for many things, you are less likely to be taken seriously. The "No" will come more frequently, and the "Yes" will come more begrudgingly.

When there's something you want, you have to make sure you have built a solid amount of goodwill with the person you want to present the request to.

Tact

The situation you pick in order to ask for something special can be key. When adults are in the middle of something stressful, or in the middle of something altogether, it is very easy to get the dismissive "No." This means that you may have to be patient and look for the right opportunity to ask for anything special you want. Down-time before bed time can be good, and down-time on weekends can also work. When you do find a good time, it's important to set the stage.

What's wrong? Dad busy, the stage was not prepared, the date is far too soon.

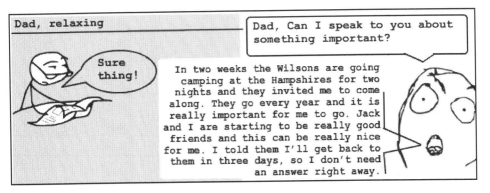

What works here: Dad relaxed. You got Dad's full attention by asking if you can ask. You shared a good amount of detail, which shows that you are responsible and understand what's important. You gave enough lead time so Dad is not put on the spot.

Start small, build credit

In life, there is one type of currency that can open almost any door for you. It's a powerful key. It's a surefire code. And, it is much simpler than you think:

The magic secret is nothing but doing what you said you would.

That is it.

No one expects you to shop for the family seven days a week, but when you said you'd pick up pasta on the way home from school, someone is counting on you.

Doing what we said we would, believe it or not, is the key to the entire economy! It is called credit.

When you have a credit card, you promise that you will pay VISA back, usually within a month or so, for buying you a pair of sneakers. If you pay it back, your credit grows, and in a year or two of paying your credit card bill, your credit grows and you can buy a car or eventually even a house!

It is all based on that simple concept: people that have the cash to buy you the house (the bank) see that, based on your past actions, you will indeed pay it back.

This same technique works at home with parents, and it works wonders.

Your parents often say, I am certain: "If you show me I can trust you, then . . ." All they mean is just that: "If I can trust you to do what we agreed that you will do, then next time you will have more freedom to do other things you want to."

The beauty of this system is that it is totally up to you! What it requires is patience.

Believe me—your parents remember! They always have a credit rating for every kid showing just how much they can be counted on.

The natural and simple process is this:

You promise you'll do something. Small, big, doesn't matter!

If you do it, your credit score rises. If you don't, or are late, then your credit score drops.

Next time you ask for privilege, it is compared with your credit score, and you either do or do not get trusted based mostly on your past ability to keep your word.

What's good about this system is that you can always start building your credit! You can always start small. Knowing that everything you do right contributes, you can make sure to do two things: First, only commit to things you know you can do, no matter how small. Second, take every commitment you make very seriously. Carry it to completion.

It is far better to promise to mow the front lawn and get it done than to commit to mulching the gardens for the entire neighborhood and never get to it.

Make sure to treat every time you borrow something as if you borrowed money from the bank. No, I don't suggest that you track it using accounting software. What I am saying is that when you borrow anything from anyone, make sure they know when you returned it. When people don't have to run after you for things you borrowed, they're much more likely to let you borrow again.

Here are some examples:

What went wrong: One transaction at a time! You can't expect to get and get without showing that you are responsible enough to return money (or things) you borrowed. It may seem harsh, but it's not. Even though it is your family, your word counts for a lot, and you want to make sure to keep to it if you want to be taken seriously.

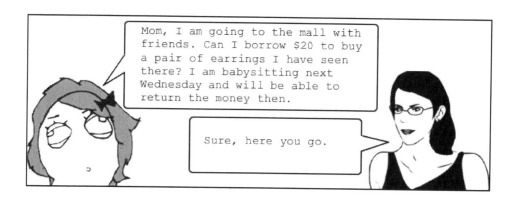

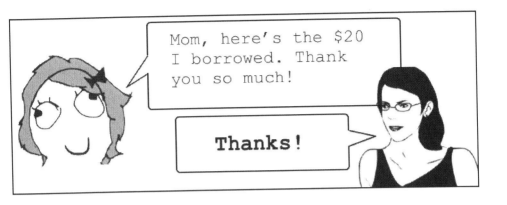

What went right: The girl asked for a small amount, and made sure to not leave any unpaid debts. The borrowed money was returned on time, and Mom is ready for the next time you ask for anything with a big, fat, "Yes."

Playing pretend

Problems around the house have the nasty habit of sticking around. Bad feelings between people are like dust: if you don't clear them out, they tend to pile up, and before you know it they become their own animal. As we have already seen, human nature is such that for the most part we prefer to blame someone else rather than own our part of the deal. We automatically become defensive and think that everyone else is to blame for how we feel.

Think about this logically for a minute—can it really be that we are right and everyone else is wrong? No, it can't.

So who is right? That's simple: the first one to let go!

Holding on to your side of an argument long after everyone involved already forgot why it even started is just a plain silly thing we all do.

The worst thing is that no matter how right we think we are, as long as we're holding a grudge, we are keeping the tension and bad feeling around the house alive. It may not be our fault that the argument started, but we are keeping it going, and it certainly is up to us to end it.

But how? Here's something fun to try: Pick one person around the house that you have been having issues with. Then, drop them! Just for a week, convince yourself that this person is the coolest around and that having them in your family is great. Refuse to take offense at anything they say. Anticipate when you'll have a fight, and calmly slip out of any situation where you may fight. Keep it up for a week or so and see what happens.

What I guarantee is that the other person will soften towards you as well, and you two will find a common language so that when things do get tense, as they are sure to get at some point, you'll have a much easier time resolving it.

What went wrong: Sure, your brother may be at fault, and may be yanking your chain. However, your angry reaction to his actions makes him want to do it again.

What went right: First, you looked at your own reaction and you felt better; that's huge!

Second, your positive reaction to your brother will eventually make him be less negative towards you.

Playing the "Compare Siblings" game

One word of advice: don't do it!

Some parents have made it a constant balancing act to make sure all their kids get exactly the same treatment. But guess what: if your parents have to constantly make sure that your sister or brother isn't getting the short end of the stick, all siblings end up with more things they don't want and less things they do.

There are two things you can do here:

Create a pact with your siblings that instead of complaining when the other one gets a special treat, you will support them and be happy for them! Why? Because the more special treatment they get that you don't, the more credit you have to ask for things that are special for you that they don't get.

Decide, hopefully with your siblings, to stop complaining about what they get that you believe is unfair! Doing that will ensure that either they will lose something and hate your guts, or you might get what they were getting just to discover that it is actually not at all what you want or like.

You and your siblings are different people and you like different things. Sometimes we all get jealous, and without thinking we try to make everything as fair as possible so that it doesn't seem that Mom and Dad like our siblings more. This never has good results. You may get something in the short term, or begrudge one of your siblings something they were getting, but you are also elevating the "yuck factor" around the house.

Try a little exercise: Next time you feel that you are getting the short end of the stick, don't jump to try and make it right. Know that your day will come, when you will be in the cozy chair. Right now, let it go. Say to your sister or brother something like, "I am really happy for you that you are getting to do that. I know how much it means to you." Can you imagine anything that will make them want to support you next time you get something that is special to you?

Your biggest allies

The people that can sometimes seem like your biggest competition and at other times the bane of your existence can be slowly turned into your best and most important allies: your siblings!

If you are the oldest, you're in luck. Your younger sibs already think you're a demigod. I know that they can make your life hell sometimes, but believe me, in some real way, there is nothing they want more in life than for you to like them and approve of them. They just want to be your friend, and while their friendship may mean more to them than to you, having them be your partner rather than your rival is critical.

If you are a younger sibling, then you have your work cut out for you. The main change you can make is to find the things that you are doing to aggravate your brother, sister, or all of them, and apologize for it. It is very difficult to actually stop behaving a certain way. If your family dynamic is such that your role is to be the annoying or hurtful brother or sister, stopping can prove elusive. A good place to start is acknowledging when you do spark trouble, and to let your victims know that you are really sorry and that you are really trying to stop, regardless of it being difficult sometimes.

Start by giving this book to your brother or sister. Or use some trusted reverse psychology: put it on your bed and tell them that this is your special book and not to read it. They are most likely going to take the bait.

Playing ping pong

When we have an argument with someone, it is almost like a ping pong game. But instead of paddles and a ball, we play it with words:

Siblings standing and talking, words flying like ping pong balls.

When we get in this mode, it is very difficult to be the one that stops the argument.

We feel that if we let go, we will lose. We would not be more wrong.

The fact is that as long as you are in the middle of a stupid argument, you both are losing. Letting go means stopping to care about winning or losing.

Letting go is choosing not to play the game. It is choosing to go and do something fun instead!

What you can and what you can't do

You cannot change other people at will. You can affect them, make them sad, happy, or angry. You can cause them to laugh, cry, or want to pull their hair out. People can sometimes change because of you, but that is very rare.

When I was younger, I totally believed that if I just said the right thing to the right person, if I could just make them see my point of view, they would surely change how they do things and see things my way. Now I know that it is habit that drives most of what people do, and people prefer what they know to anything you can tell them.

What you can do is change your relationship with people. You can change how people relate to you and perceive you. You can change how much fun it is to be around you, and therefore change how much fun you have being around the same people.

The way you respond to situations, as you saw in this chapter, can determine how good your day-to-day life is and how much freedom you get.

7

Working your magic

*"Imagination is everything. It is the preview
of life's coming attractions." Albert Einstein*

You must have been told that you "have to believe in yourself" about a million times. But what exactly does it mean?

Unfortunately, this thing we can do, believe in ourselves, has turned into something people say.

Lets take a few minutes and break it down. Lets see what believing in yourself means, what it can do for you, and how to start doing it.

The non-reality reality

Being grounded in reality seems to be one of the most important things for people. "Losing it" is often associated with someone who has created his or her own reality in their mind. But is this as far as the story goes? Is there really a single reality, and we are all part of it?

It is not that simple.

Please know that I will not be going on about some hypothetical science-fiction take on reality. What I am discussing here is very real and has a profound impact of our lives.

Some twenty five hundred years ago, the Greek philosopher Democritus came up with the idea that everything in the world was made of tiny, indivisible building blocks called atoms. Much like LegoLand where everything is made of Lego blocks, in our reality, he thought, everything is made of those atoms. He figured that the property of the atom would determine the property of the material that was made of those atoms.

He was right, but only part right.

What Democritus didn't realize is that not only can the atom be broken down into components such as protons and electrons, but that when you look closely into each and every element of an atom, what you find is . . . drum roll . . . nothing! Well, nothing solid, at least. What later scientists found was that the basic building blocks of everything in the universe are just energy. Imagine that!

About 100 years ago, an entire new branch of science started, called quantum physics. Quantum physicists are continuing to make amazing discoveries that don't always mesh with what scientists believed was possible. For example, quantum physics shows us that the building blocks of the universe show different characteristics when they are being watched! That's right: when you observe an atom, parts inside of it act differently than they would if you weren't watching.

This paints a very different reality than the one we previously believed in. Before, we believed that the universe was made of solid matter, liquid and gas, and we were separate entities roaming this material-based world. Now we know that reality isn't as much what's there, but rather our perception of what's there.

But we all perceive things so differently!

Right! This is why our realities are so different from one another.

What belief is

Belief is how we know things to be. For example, you believe that you can't fly, right? You also believe that you can make a peanut-butter sandwich.

So what? This is just reality, right? Doesn't everyone know that?

Yes, but what about other things, such as whether you can win a tennis match, learn how to play guitar, or find someone who will go on a date with you?

There are things in your life that you want, but do you also believe, deep inside, that you can have them?

We tend to think that believing things are real comes **after** they appear in reality, but quite the opposite is the truth: Your reality is created, constantly, based on the very basic things that you believe.

Come again?

I know, there are no kindergarten books that illustrate that point, so I'll say it again: your reality is created, constantly, based on the very basic things that you believe.

Hmm . . . now this puts a whole new twist on you believing in yourself, doesn't it! This means that believing you can do something is not only related to how well you can do it, but is actually required for you to be able to do something!

In short, believing that something is possible is the first and most important thing you can do in order to achieve that thing. The difference is that believing is something you do inside your mind! There is no 200 pound rock blocking it, there is no concrete wall you have to dig through, there are no people telling you that you can't. Believing happens in your mind, and your mind only.

So what is there to stop you from believing? Simple: things you already believe. See, from the day we are born, we start to collect information based on what we experience. After a while, that information becomes cemented in our mind, and we tend to believe that it is just how things are. In fact, it is mostly just beliefs! Beliefs are not bad. For example, believing that we can get seriously hurt if we fall from the roof causes us to keep our distance form the edge of the building. We can also have beliefs that have no relation to our everyday life at all. But what about our everyday lives? What about the many things we are involved in like school, sports, friends?

In those cases, our beliefs play a huge role in what we can easily do, and what we just can't seem to be able to or are too discouraged to even try.

Think about this for a minute: If you believed that there is no way you could do something, would you even attempt it? Probably not.

Remember our friend, the subconscious? Our subconscious actually focuses on what we believe when it makes things happen or not happen for us.

For example, you can easily make a sandwich without even noticing. You do that because your subconscious is doing it for you. You have no doubt that you can do it, and therefore the subconscious has no barriers.

Other things that you find really difficult work the same way: your doubt in your ability to do them tells your subconscious to put the brakes on.

Changing what we believe

So, now that you know all of this, doing anything will be easy; all you have to do is believe you can, right?

Mmm . . . not exactly.

You see, replacing deep negative beliefs with positive new ones can be difficult. Your subconscious didn't accumulate those beliefs over night, and it's not about to let go of them that quickly.

But this doesn't mean that those negative beliefs cannot be slowly chipped away. Once the process of change has started, it will become easier to continue. Every bit of change that happens in your belief will slowly affect your reality in a real way.

How?

To know how to change your beliefs, we should first look at how beliefs are created, and how they are reinforced.

We sometimes tend to think that problems that were created in our lives were created long ago, and we have to know why they happened in order to fix them. Not so. Our problems may have originated from something that happened long ago, but their existence today is due to our constant reinforcement of them. We do that with our thoughts, most of which are automatic.

My thoughts are not me!

Thoughts have the nasty habit of speaking in first person. When a thought you have starts with "I," it tells you something about yourself, but it is not the truth. Instead, it is something you have come to believe.

Lets take the thought, "I am not good enough for the varsity soccer team." This thought may pop into your head when you see a signup sheet for the team, or randomly during the day. Does it actually mean that you don't have the talent to be on that team? That one of your legs is seven inches shorter than the other, and they don't allow that? It means nothing. It is an automatic tape playing in your head that is based on your belief—a limiting belief, at that.

So if the thought is not me, who am I?

Ah! Good question. I'm glad I asked.

You are the one that has the ability to observe the thought!

Lets try it. Right now, close your eyes and watch your thoughts as if they were passing through your head. Really, do it—this is not optional. OK, here we go. You're going to close your eyes and wait for a thought to pass through. Since we don't control most of the thoughts we have, it shouldn't take long. As soon as a thought passes through, observe it! Say to yourself, "Hmm... I just had a thought that told me that _____."

Eyes closed . . . thinking . . . observing. You're not off the hook on this one until you do it!

OK, now that you caught a thought and looked at it, we can make the distinction:

The thought you observed came from your subconscious, and the observation came from you!

When you get a negative thought, then, it is not you. You are responsible for the next two steps: 1) Observe or look at the thought (you need to think about the thought); and 2) React to it! Either buy it or not. Here's how:

This is how most people relate to their thoughts:

This is how you can change your beliefs:

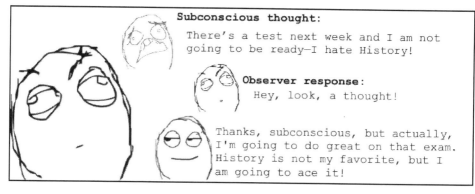

See, you may think (in this made-up scenario) that you fear history tests because you failed one before. The fact is that while you started to fear history tests when you failed, you still fear them because your automatic thoughts reinforce that fear, and you believe them.

It is time to start listening to your own thoughts and stop believing them right away!

8

School drama

"You can get all A's and still
flunk life" Walker Percy

Unless you are either home schooled or raised by wolves, you go to school. I will spare you the speech about how important it is that you stay in school and work hard for your grades—there are other people that already do plenty of that. Instead, I want to look at other, more interesting aspects of being in school.

Being successful at school

We all know what that means, don't we? Good grades! Getting good grades gets everyone off of your back. Teachers don't pick on you as much and your parents are happy.

When your grades are down, on the other hand, everybody is down, and you are the target.

Lets try to make sense of it all.

To start, a normal school in the United States recognizes a very specific set of abilities that not all kids have! Forcing everyone to be good at everything in school is like having many differently shaped pegs but having holes with only one shape. The pegs that fit are happy, the ones that almost fit are barely squeezed in, and others get completely disregarded as failures. They are not failures; they are just good at other things! Some kids are good at sports or music or art, some kids are amazing storytellers, some can run forever. Some are even good at math and history, but get really stressed before exams and can't remember anything. Tough luck for them.

Knowing that, what can *you* do to make your life in school more manageable?

First, know your strengths, and your limitations. You were not meant to be able to know and do everything. Figure out what things you are good at and what you like to do. They might be things you can do at school, and they might not. The idea here is not to ignore what you don't like. The idea is to develop your strengths and manage your weaknesses. This means studying as hard as you can, but not getting too stressed about outscoring everyone in every subject. You want to put your best efforts behind the subjects you love, and stress less about other subjects.

Either way, listing them out is a good idea.

First, write down the subjects that you like and are good at, and make another list of subjects that are not your strength.

Second, create your own scale of success. It can mean that you will be okay with C's in some subjects but A's in others.

Third, share your plan and get agreement. It is important not to go against your parents on this one.

Explain to your parents that you just can't be good at every subject, and that you want to work on areas where you feel more talented. Promise your parents and/or teachers that you will work even harder in these subjects, but that you want to be given some slack on the subjects that don't interest you that much.

If you think it's a good idea, you may want to ask your parents what subjects they remember from school—maybe tidbits from one or two. Explain that it is more important to you to be great at one or two things than to be just okay at more subjects.

If you believe it, they should support you on that.

Other kids

In school and in general, other kids can be a lot of fun, they can be great friends, and they can also be a royal pain in the butt. Knowing how to deal with kids can make your life that much better.

Friends

There are two kinds of friends: those who are your friend because you make them look good, and those who are your friend because they make you feel good.

Sometimes we try so hard to be friends with kids who are considered cool that we forget the point of having friends in the first place.

True friends never want you to do things you're uncomfortable with. True friends just make you feel good! True friends are your friends because they like to hang out with exactly who it is you are.

Not that you or your friends can't be cool, but once in a while it can be helpful for us to assess our friends. We can start with the simple things—how they make us feel! When you think about a particular friend, what is the first thing that comes to your mind? Fun? Stress? Dread? Excitement? That you are being used?

Every relationship has its time. There are people who are a good fit for you during a certain time, and then they can either stay or fall of the map. It's important to evaluate friends once in a while and see just how important they are to you.

If one or more of your friends make you uncomfortable, or ask you to do things that make you uncomfortable, it is definitely time to think about spending less time with them. Sometimes, we hang around with people just because we believe that no one else would want to hang around with us. That, I can tell you, is not at all true. Lets look at that a bit closer.

Being yourself

Sometimes, when going to school, one of the toughest things to be is ourselves! We're afraid that if we show who we really are we will be made fun of. So in order to survive, we pick up little things that we see other kids do, and we do them in order to fit in.

Finding ways to fit in is perfectly fine! It's natural and can have good results. However, we must always make sure to be mostly ourselves. This is because no matter how different or quirky you are, the only way you will make real friends is when they see the real you. The real you is the coolest, because it is authentic, and not trying to copy anyone!

You have to know that not everyone will appreciate the real you. That's perfectly okay! You don't *want* everyone to appreciate you. You would have to be rather boring in order to have everyone appreciated you. More than that, anyone who appreciates you for being the most *you* that you can be will like you much more than they would if you were a vanilla version of yourself, aiming to please everyone.

No matter who we are, how we look, how big or small, plus-size or tiny, there are other kids in our school or area who would love to hang out with us!

Next time you go shopping for clothes, ask yourself what *you* like to wear, rather than what you think will be approved by the "cool" kids. Whenever you make decisions based on whether other kids will approve or not, think again. This is your life, you cannot change who you are, and you especially shouldn't change who you are for the sake of people who you don't really like in the first place.

Hear me now, and hear me good: the coolest you can be is authentic. Yourself. Who you are. Do things that make you happy, hang out with people who make you happy, and if anyone gives you a hard time about it, send them to me—I'll give them an earful.

How many friends do you need?

Really, one or two true friends who have your back is great! More is good too, but we are not measured by how many friends we have. What's more, once we find that friend, nothing else really matters! Getting into trouble is not as bad, fighting with your parents is not as bad, and being sad is not as bad. When you have one or two people you can trust and share your experience with, life is just that much better.

Be yourself, and before you know it that friend will appear from the most unexpected place!

Bullies

Every school has one or two. Bullies prove the theory that a few people can mess things up for everyone. They are scary. They can hurt and torment.

What you have to know is that the story of school bullies is not one with an easily recognizable bad guy and a victim.

Yes, I agree, the little kid getting beat up is for the most part the victim. However, before we label the bully as the bad guy, we need to look at all sides of the story.

What we have to realize is that no one is born a bully. For someone to become a bully, they have to endure first hand a lot of the same scary things that they do to other people. In short, bullies are victims, too. It is easy for us to hate them and blame them for everything, but the fact is that they suffer from the way they behave all of the time.

What? Bullies are the ones that suffer? But they are nothing but bullies!

No, they are not. Bullies are people just like you and me. They turned to that behavior because someone, possibly at home, was hurting them. It is still their responsibility to stop their hurtful action, but we have to be aware of what they are going through. For the most part, when bullies hurt, all they really do is say: "I am really hurting! Please, someone notice and love me. Sorry, but this is the only way I know how to behave!"

The third part of the story of bullies, besides the kid that is doing the pounding and the one being pounded, are the rest of the kids! Everyone else gets to see a really bad situation, and for the most part, not get a really good example of how to deal with it. If the bullies get punished, then they don't get the help they need. If they don't get punished, then no one gets helped. Some adults simply don't know how to handle difficult situations like that, so they either pretend not to notice or say things like, "Boys will be boys," or "It's best if they learn to resolve it themselves."

People don't act up because they are bad. People act up because it's the only way they know how to say: "Pay attention! My life is not going well, and I need some help!"

9

Food, fitness, and What it Means to Us

"There is no money in healthy
people or dead people. The money
is in sick people." -Bill Maher

When we think about being sick and healthy, we usually think about diseases making us sick, and doctors giving us medicine to make us healthy. This is not even the half of the story.

The real story is food! Yes, what you eat and drink, for the most part, is what makes you either healthy or sick, fat or not.

You may think that what you eat is not really your choice.

But if you believe, as I do, that what you put into your body is one of the most important considerations you can make in your day, then know this: you have a lot of say over what you eat! You can help educate your school and family about what food does to us, and you can change some really bad eating habits that many people growing up in America have.

Food doesn't only affect your health and your body. Food also affects your mood and your focus. It can make you depressed or help you concentrate and ace the exam.

The main problem with food is that it becomes a habit that's rather difficult to break. When you say you like eating something and hate eating something else, what you are actually saying is that you got used to eating one thing, and got used to avoiding the other food. What we like to eat is not really a part of who we are—it is only a habit! And when you decide a habit you have is hurting you in some way, then it is a habit worth breaking!

While the food subject is big enough for several books, lets look at some fundamental things that can help you when you choose what things you put in your mouth.

What is processed food?

Processed food is simply food that has been processed. Most food we eat is processed in some way.

The opposite of processed food is whole food. Eating an apple or carrot is eating whole food. Eating a baked yam is also eating whole food.

So, is processed food bad? It depends just how processed it is. Lets take a closer look.

Have you ever eaten fries, a burger, or chicken nuggets at a fast food restaurant? You probably have. Those fast foods I mentioned are probably the most processed foods you can eat. And what does that mean? It means that the amount of processing it got along the way to look and taste like it does made it no longer have any of the texture, taste, color, or nutrition of its original ingredients. At some point in the process, each one of the three foods I mentioned here was a completely flavorless, colorless, odorless paste. White paste with absolutely nothing that you need in your body. On the other hand, it has a lot of things you really want to avoid, but that's for later.

When you eat junk food, you are eating white paste with flavor, odor, and color added to it, which was pressed by a machine into the shape it has now in order to make you want to eat it. Then, it is fried and made to taste so irresistible that when we see a billboard or a commercial on TV advertising it, we want nothing more than to bite into it.

So what is wrong with some fast food once in a while? It's not so much a matter of "what's wrong"—that is for you to decide. I can share with you a few things that it does to your body, and you can make up your own mind.

To start, fast food is really fatty. Even the salads you get in those places have dressing so fattening that it can put a burger to shame.

Eating fast food makes you overweight, it makes you groggy, and worst of all—it makes you want more! That's right: fast food is proven to be as addictive as drugs! Can you imagine that? Not only is it really bad for us, but it makes us need it.

All of this makes fast food a really difficult habit to break. But if you feel strongly enough about it, you have more power than you think! Look up studies—that's what Google is for! Suggest to your parents that next time you go out, go to another place. There are many restaurants that serve honest food that your whole family can appreciate. If you come to Mom or Dad with the hard facts abut fast food, and tell them that you want to start eating more healthy, they are more likely to be impressed then to give you a hard time.

Your body is growing and developing, and what you eat now can have implications for your long-term health. Take charge. Be your own person. If it is important to you to eat more healthily, then find a way to make it happen!

Food from animals

You might still be young enough to remember the first time you made the connection between the food people call chicken, and the animal called chicken. Remember when you realized that pork is actually a piece of a pig, and that beef or steak is actually a cow? If not, it may be better. After all, it can be a bit of a shock.

What you probably heard in school is that meat is important because it gives up protein we need, and that milk and dairy are good for calcium. It is not a surprise, since the meat and dairy industries are the ones that supply schools with the nutritional information that is then given to you.

Let me be as clear about it as I can possibly be: both of those things are not only untrue, but they are lies. They are nasty, dirty lies, and their intention is to have us all consume more of those products.

To start, regular food we eat every day has more than enough protein for our bodies. We do not need meat for it. And calcium? Milk does have calcium, but it is not in a form that can be absorbed by our body. Does it make sense to you that humans would need food that was meant for baby calves? It doesn't make sense to me.

We are taught that humans are carnivores or omnivores,[7] but that is not true either. Humans are designed in every way to be plant eaters. We are not fast or strong enough to catch animals, we don't have the right teeth for tearing flesh, and new studies show that meat is responsible for heart diseases, strokes, and cancer. Humans can eat meat, but for the most part, it is not a very good idea.

What many people don't talk about is that besides making us fat on the outside, meat and dairy cause real damage on the inside. It is known to build plaque in our blood vessels that eventually can cause strokes and cardiovascular diseases.

Many people associate eating meat with being strong. The opposite is true. Many athletes are vegans or vegetarians,[8] and eating too much meat is known for making us fat and tired, not strong.

Acne

Acne is an unavoidable problem many of us suffer from. There are many creams and remedies that can help reduce it. Nothing, however, can help you treat to this problem as

---

7   *Carnivores are meat eaters, and omnivores are animals that eat both plants and meat.*
8   *Vegetarians don't eat meat, and vegans don't eat anything that came from an animal, including dairy.*

cheaply, easily, and effectively as making better food choices. It has been proven that dairy (milk, cheese, etc.) is a big contributor to acne.

If you suffer from acne, I urge you to cut down dairy as much as possible. I know, pizza is so darn delicious! Changing what you eat is a choice that you can start to make. For example, you can decide to totally avoid milk and cheese for three weeks. Tell your parents and anyone else you eat around that this is your plan, and stick to it. It is much easier to stick to a three weeks plan than to a "from now on" plan.

Try almond, soy, and rice milk, and pick the one that taste best to you. The vanilla flavored ones are actually really delicious! Find a local pizza place that makes vegan pizza. No, it's not your usual pizza, but this is where your priorities kick in. Pizza is something you eat once in a while—your body is something that is carrying you and representing you 24 hours a day, seven days a week.

Also, cut down on sugar as much as possible. Using the newest, most expensive acne cream may work, but it only works after the problem already happened! Changing what you eat has the potential to both reverse the problem and prevent it in the future.[9]

Sugar

Sugar and corn syrup are everywhere! And why? Farmers get money from the government for producing corn syrup, so food makers can get it for cheap. This is the rea-

---

9   *For more information go to: www.naturalnews.com, and search for "Four Ways Milk Causes Acne."*

son why it is in so many foods, not because it is any good. In fact, it is horrible! It makes us tired and overweight.

Sugar is not only in candy and desserts, but also in drinks. Did you know that every ten cans of Coke or Pepsi contain an entire can of sugar?

Remember: you are ultimately responsible for your own health. Take charge! Look at the back of the cans, look at the labels of your morning cereal, and see how much sugar it has. After that, go shopping with your parents and help them make good food choices. You have the power to do that, and your parents will most likely be very supportive.

Now, there is nothing wrong with indulging with a good dessert! Desserts are just that: something yummy, sugary, and sweet that we have once in a while. I love desserts, and the more sugary, the better. What we want to watch for are foods that are supposed to be healthy and good, like break-fast cereal or sports drinks, that instead are filled with sugar.

Diet and energy drinks

No, diet drinks are not going to make you thin. Diet drinks are, in some ways, worse than the non-diet ones.

Don't even get me started on energy drinks. Those drinks are like drugs. Search Google for "Energy drink effect on kids," find a good article, and read it.

Here's an excerpt from an article on abcnews.com by Liz Neporent, ABC News Medical Unit:

Members of the men's swim team at Midlakes High School in Rochester, N.Y., would often complain of feeling dizzy, shaky and hyper during practice; sometimes they'd vomit in the middle of a workout.

Coach R.C. Weston knew their sickness wasn't related to lack of conditioning or overtraining. "It was directly related to their consumption of energy drinks," he said.

The swimmers admitted that downing an energy drink before practice didn't help their performance—in fact they were left feeling unfocused and dehydrated—but they drank them anyway because they "taste amazing" and the "heightened sensation makes you feel more energetic." Team members are now banned from drinking them while in training.

Downing cans of this crazy stuff doesn't make you cool, it makes you sick. If you want to be cool, do your own thing. Be your own person. Make decisions that are different from what's considered cool.

If you want to drink something healthy, drink water!

Being picky

Some kids are pickier than others. Watch yourself as you become confined to a smaller and smaller variety of foods you're willing to eat. Make a commitment to try a new food once a week—it is so much fun! It may be a bit scary, but there's so much amazing stuff out there. Staying confined to mac and cheese is kids stuff—snap out of it. :-)

Changing your menu

Even after you realize what foods you do or do not want to eat, making changes can take time. Some of us can make a decision to stop eating certain things, like becoming a vegetarian or vegan, and manage to just make the switch. For most of us it is a much slower, longer road.

If your path leads you towards a new kind of food, or away from another kind, then allow yourself to take it a step at a time. Remind yourself why you want to make the change, and get your parents on board. From there, you can achieve anything.

Cardio is the miracle drug

In his book *Spark*, Dr. John Ratey describes the science that shows how simply getting your heart rate up by running one mile a few times a week, can grow brain cells, make you think clearer, do better on tests, help get rid of depression, anxiety and other mental and physical symptoms. And as we all know, also make you more fit and confident .

In *Spark*, Dr. Ratey follows a class in Naplerville, a suburb of Chicago, where the students improved their math and science scores to become the highest ranked class in the entire world. How did they do it? By getting their heart rate up on a regular basis.

I know changing habits is tough, but if you're ready for a real physical and mental boost, then put on running shorts and run four laps around the track as fast as you can. It's scientifically proven, and best of all, it is free and has no side effects.

10

Conclusion

If there is one thing I want you to know better than any-thing else, it is that this life you live here along with all of us is yours. It is not your parents' or your teacher's, it is not for the sake of the economy or anything else.

This life is yours, and you were meant to be happy. You were meant to go out and create, whatever it is you create. You are here to experience and share your unique perspec-tive. You are a good, capable human, and anything that stands in your way can be slowly melted away.

I am here to tell you to own your life. Complaining, blaming, and making excuses are all automated messages that keep on interrupting it. You can't stop them altogether, but it is your duty to observe them. Tell them: "Thanks, but no thanks!"

I am here to tell you to dream up an amazing life for yourself. Find what you love to do, then find someone that believes in you, and shoot for the stars!

You can, you can,
and then you
can some more.

Now, give life a
big hug, and
go on
your journey.

50761251R00065

Made in the USA
Charleston, SC
08 January 2016